Our Earth

Rocks and Soil

Jen Green

PowerKiDS
press.

New York

Published in 2008 by The Rosen Publishing Group, Inc.
29 East 21st Street, New York, NY 10010

First Edition

Picture credits:
Cover Dreamstime.com/Stuart Elflett, 1 Dreamstime.com, 4 Dreamstime.com/ Rebecca Abell, 5 Dreamstime.com/Eric Foltz, 6 Digital Vision, 7t Dreamstime.com/Andy Butler, 7m Dreamstime.com, 7b Dreamstime.com, 8 Dreamstime.com, 9 Dreamstime.com/Stuart Elflett, 10 Dreamstime.com/Ricardo Garza, 11 Dreamstime.com/N. Joy Neish, 12 Dreamstime.com/Scott Rothstein, 13 Dreamstime.com/Alexander Maksimov, 14 Dreamstime.com/Mark Bond, 15 Corbis/Didier Dutheil/Sygma, 16 Digital Vision, 17 Alamy/Stephen Barnett/ImageState, 18 Dreamstime.com, 19 Ecoscene/Peter Hulme, 20 Dreamstime.com/Pavel Gribkov, 21 courtesy of John Deere

Produced by Tall Tree Ltd.
Editor: Jon Richards
Designer: Ben Ruocco
Consultant: John Williams

Library of Congress Cataloging-in-Publication Data

Green, Jen.
  Rocks and soil / Jen Green. — 1st ed.
      p. cm. — (Our Earth)
  Includes index.
  ISBN 978-1-4042-4271-5 (library binding)
  1. Rocks—Juvenile literature. 2. Soils—Juvenile literature. I. Title.

QE432.2.G74 2008
552—dc22
                                        2007032599

Manufactured in China

Contents

What are rocks?

Rocks are the solid materials that make up the Earth. These solid pieces of rock are broken up over time, and mix with plant and animal remains to form soil.

❤ Beach sand is made of tiny bits of rock and shell.

Rocks come in many shapes and sizes. Cliff faces and boulders are large pieces of rock. Sand and gravel are tiny pieces. Rocks may be hard, like granite, or soft, like chalk.

Mountains are made from huge pieces of rock that have been pushed high into the air.

How are rocks made?

There are three main types of rock. **Volcanic** rocks, such as granite, form when hot, melted rock flows out of a **volcano**, and then cools and hardens.

Liquid **lava** comes from deep under the Earth's surface.

⬣ Chalk is a secondhand rock that is made from tiny pieces of shell.

⬣ Granite is a volcanic rock.

Chalk and sandstone are "secondhand" rocks. They form when pieces of rock or shell on the seabed are squashed into layers. Marble and slate are "changed" rocks. They form when other rocks are squashed or heated deep under the ground.

⬣ Marble is a changed rock that is made when limestone is squashed underground.

Rocks and the weather

Wind, water, and ice wear down rocks. Frost and ice can break rocks into pieces. Wind and rain can carve smooth shapes into rocks.

The Grand Canyon has been shaped by the flow of the Colorado river.

Rivers and icy **glaciers** bash and scrape against rocks on the surface. This carves large holes into the rock, which are called valleys and canyons.

⬇ Waves beating against this seashore have shaped these cliffs and rock pillars.

Using rocks

We dig rocks out of the ground at mines and **quarries** and use them to make things. Hard rocks, such as granite, are used to build houses and roads.

❯❯ Marble is another hard rock that is used in buildings such as the Texas Capitol.

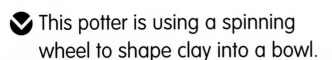 This potter is using a spinning wheel to shape clay into a bowl.

Soft rocks are also useful. Cement is made using limestone. Soft, black graphite is used to make lead for pencils. Moist, squishy clay is shaped to make bricks and pottery, and then baked in an oven to make it hard.

Metals and gems

Gold, silver, and iron are **metals** found in rocks. Mixtures of rocks and metals are called **ores**. Iron ore is melted in a hot **furnace** to separate the iron from the rock.

Pieces of gold are dug out of the ground in mines, or they are found in rivers.

Some rocks contain **gems**, such as diamonds and rubies. These gems are dug out of the ground in mines and separated from the rock. They are then cut and polished so that they sparkle.

This piece of rock contains pieces of the gem topaz. When it is cut and polished, topaz can be clear, yellow, brown, blue, or pink.

Fossils

Fossils are the remains of animals or plants that have turned into rock. After these plants and animals died, their remains were buried by rocks and soil and slowly turned into rock over millions of years.

This is an ammonite fossil. Ammonites were shellfish that lived in the oceans millions of years ago.

Fact

The oldest fossils ever found are the remains of tiny creatures called **bacteria** that are 3.5 billion years old.

Fossils remain buried until scientists dig them up. The fossils may have broken up beneath the ground. Scientists then have to put the fossil pieces together carefully, to find out what the plant or animal looked like.

▲ These scientists are removing soil to uncover the fossil of a dinosaur's leg bone.

Fossil fuels

Coal, oil, and gas are called **fossil fuels**. They are the remains of plants or animals that lived millions of years ago. These remains are buried under layers of rocks and soil.

❯❯ Oil rigs pump oil and gas from beneath the ocean floor.

Fact

Oil is also used to make paint, plastic, and fertilizer.

We burn fossil fuels in **power stations** to produce electricity. Cars, buses, and trains run on diesel or gasoline, which are made from oil.

Coal is mined using drills and special cutting machines.

17

Soil

Soil is made from tiny pieces of rock that have been broken down by the weather. Soil can be chalky, sandy, or like peat, depending on the type of rock it was made from.

❯❯ Crumbly **peat** is the best type of soil to use for potted plants.

Fact

A thin layer of soil can take hundreds of years to form.

Soil is formed in layers. The top layer of soil contains rich, dark **humus**, made from rotting leaves. The layers below contain larger stones, and at the bottom is solid rock.

⬣ You can see the layers of soil in this picture.

Living in the soil

Soil contains the remains of plants and animals. These add nourishing **minerals** to the soil. Plants and trees use these nourishing minerals and water.

⬇ Many small animals live in the soil, eating plants. These attract larger animals, such as moles.

Animals that live in the soil include moles, rabbits, and small creatures, such as worms, slugs, and beetles. When plants and animals die, their bodies break down, adding more minerals to the soil, so that more plants can grow.

Farmers grow **crops** in the soil to provide food.

Fact

One square yard of soil contains millions of living things, but most are too small to see!

Activities

Sinking in sand

Sand is made from tiny pieces of rock, which make it very soft. See how far thick and thin objects sink into sand with this activity.

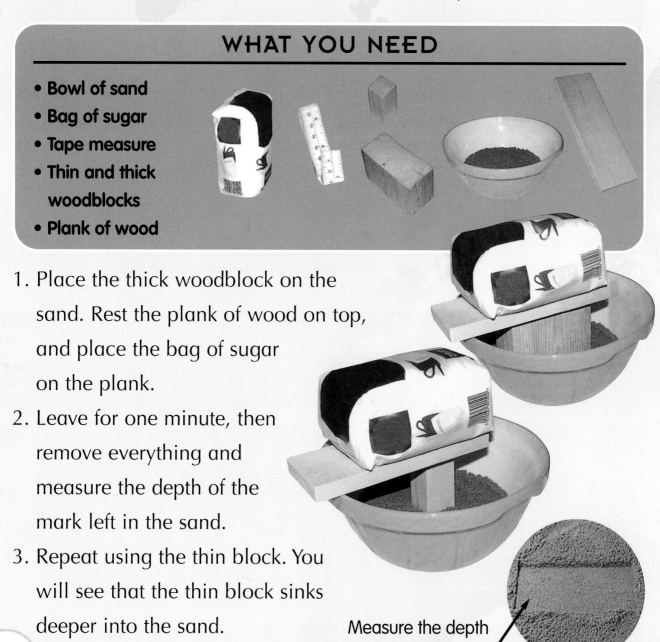

WHAT YOU NEED

- Bowl of sand
- Bag of sugar
- Tape measure
- Thin and thick woodblocks
- Plank of wood

1. Place the thick woodblock on the sand. Rest the plank of wood on top, and place the bag of sugar on the plank.

2. Leave for one minute, then remove everything and measure the depth of the mark left in the sand.

3. Repeat using the thin block. You will see that the thin block sinks deeper into the sand.

Measure the depth of each "footprint."

Rock freezing

Use this activity to see how the weather can break apart pieces of rock.

WHAT YOU NEED

- One rock
- Foil tray
- Jug of water
- Freezer
- Magnifying glass

1. Place the piece of rock in the tray and cover it with water from the jug.
2. Put the tray in the freezer and leave it for a day.
3. Take the tray out of the freezer and let the ice melt.
4. Pour the water out and rub your finger across the rock's surface. You might find that small pieces of grit are rubbed off. The cold from the freezer has broken up the rock's surface, making it crumble.

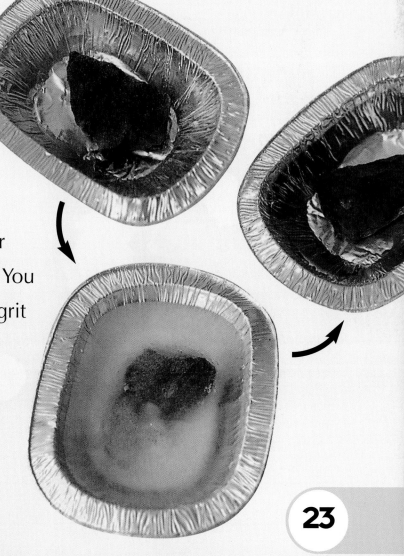

Glossary

Bacteria Tiny living things that are too small to see with the naked eye.

Crops Plants that are grown by farmers for food.

Fossil fuels Fuels that are made from the remains of plants or animals that lived millions of years ago.

Furnace A very hot fire that is used to melt metal.

Gems Minerals that can be cut or polished to make a jewel.

Glaciers Large bodies of ice.

Humus A layer of rich, dark material in the soil.

Lava Super-hot rock that has melted and flows out of a volcano and across the ground.

Metals Solid materials that are usually hard and shiny, such as iron and gold.

Minerals The solid substances from which rocks are made.

Ores Rocks or minerals that contain a metal.

Peat A type of soil that is very crumbly.

Power stations Places that produce electricity.

Quarries Places where rocks are dug from the ground.

Volcanic To do with volcanoes.

Volcano A weak point in Earth's crust through which lava flows when the volcano erupts.

Index

Web Sites
Due to the changing nature of Internet links, PowerKids Press has developed an online list of Web sites related to the subject of this book. This site is regularly updated. Please use this link to access this list:
www.powerkidslinks.com/earth/rocksoil